LOOM KNITTING
for Mommy & Me

3

6

10

12

16

22

24

LOOM KNITTING
for Mommy & Me

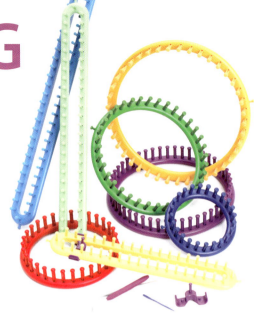

Kathy Norris

This book is your guide to creating special gifts for all the moms, babies, and children in your life! It's the newest loom knitting pattern collection by designer Kathy Norris. It includes hats, socks, mitts, a hooded scarf, a cowl, a baby jacket, and a sock monkey pillow — a total of 10 happy designs!

CHECK OUT MORE GREAT
LOOM KNITTING by Kathy Norris

Item #5604

Big Book of Loom Knitting

This 96-page book offers all the basic instructions and includes a blanket with sleeves, a felted tote, and mitts that convert to handwarmers. The cute sock monkey pocket-scarf and hat set are a perfect match for the monkey pillow in *Loom Knitting for Mommy & Me*.

Item #5250

I Can't Believe I'm Loom Knitting!

If you are new to loom knitting, this book takes you through all the basics while you make one-of-a-kind gifts. The 18 fun projects include a sampler afghan and matching pillow that teach a wide selection of stitches.

Item #4411

More Knitting Wheel Fashions

Kathy's first loom-knitting book shows you how to change colors, create I-cord, fringe-as-you-go, and make short rows while you complete mitts, slippers, socks, a baby blanket, or a wrap sweater.

Collect all 4 of Kathy's books at LeisureArts.com. Kathy Norris blogs at KathyNorrisDesigns.com.

ANKLETS

When cool weather arrives, these toasty socks will be a treat to wear around the house.

 INTERMEDIATE

SHOPPING LIST

Yarn (Medium Weight) 4 MEDIUM

[3.5 ounces, 209 yards
(100 grams, 191 meters) per skein]:

☐ 1 skein

☐ Waste yarn - small amount

Loom (Straight)

☐ 26 Pegs

Additional Supplies

☐ Knitting loom tool

☐ Yarn needle

SIZE INFORMATION

Finished Size:

6½" (16.5 cm) foot circumference and
7½{8½-9¼}"/19{21.5-23.5} cm foot
length

Size Note: We have printed the
instructions for the sizes in different
colors to make it easier for you to find:
7½" (19 cm) foot length in blue
8½" (21.5 cm) foot length in pink
9¼" (23.5 cm) foot length in green
Instructions in black apply to all sizes.

GAUGE INFORMATION

In Stockinette Stitch
(knit every row/rnd),
    16 stitches and 24 rows/rnds =
    4" (10 cm)

INSTRUCTIONS

This sock is a toe up pattern and uses
waste yarn for the provisional cast
on. The Toe is worked in rows until
the shaping is complete. The waste
yarn will be removed and the Toe
completed.

PROVISIONAL CAST ON

Using waste yarn, working as flat
knitting, and beginning with peg 1
(see diagram below), e-wrap cast on
14 pegs counter-clockwise.

E-wrap knit 3 rows.

Cut waste yarn.

TOE SHAPING

Use the knit stitch (instead of the
e-wrap knit stitch) throughout.

Rows 1 and 2: With sock color,
knit across.

The Toe shaping is achieved by
📹 working in short rows, formed by
working across only some of the pegs.
Wrap the peg indicated *(Figs. 10a & b,
page 30)*, then reverse the direction
you are working at the end of the
instructions for each row, leaving the
remaining pegs unworked.

Row 3: Bringing the working yarn to
the inside of the loom, 📹 skip 1
(Fig. 9, page 30), knit across to last
2 pegs, wrap next peg.

Refer to the diagram for the numbering system used in this pattern.

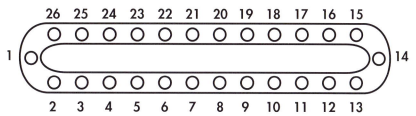

Row 4: K 10, wrap next peg.

Row 5: K9, wrap next peg.

Row 6: K8, wrap next peg.

Row 7: K7, wrap next peg.

Row 8: K6, wrap next peg.

Row 9: K5, wrap next peg.

Row 10: K4, wrap next peg.

To knit a wrapped peg, knit the peg by lifting all loops over the working yarn and off the peg. **When wrapping a peg more than once**, lift the top loop from the peg and place the wrap **above** the last one, then put the loop back onto the peg. **When knitting a peg with multiple wraps**, the loops can be lifted off, one at a time, from the bottom to the top.

Row 11: K5, wrap next peg.

Row 12: K6, wrap next peg.

Row 13: K7, wrap next peg.

Row 14: K8, wrap next peg.

Row 15: K9, wrap next peg.

Row 16: K 10, wrap next peg.

Row 17: K 12.

Row 18: K 14.

Row 19: K 13.

Lift up the bottom edge toward the inside of loom and place the loops from the first row of sock color on the pegs, placing the end stitches on pegs 1 and 14 and remaining stitches on the empty pegs *(Figs. 7a & b, page 29)*; remove waste yarn: 26 pegs used.

Row 20: Continuing to work in the same direction as the previous row, knit across to peg 1.

FOOT

Place a scrap piece of yarn around peg 1 to mark the beginning of a round.

Begin working as circular knitting.

Knit 32{38-42} rounds.

HEEL
Begin working in short rows.

Row 1: K 13, wrap next peg.

Row 2: K 12, wrap next peg.

Row 3: K 11, wrap next peg.

Rows 4-16: Work same as Toe, Rows 4-16.

Row 17: K 11, wrap next peg.

Row 18: K 12, wrap next peg.

Row 19: K 25.

RIBBING
Begin working as circular knitting.

Rnd 1: Knit next peg and lift all loops over working yarn and off peg, P1, (K1, P1) around.

Rnds 2-13: (K1, P1) around.

Work sewn bind off *(Figs. 12a & b, page 31)*.

Repeat for second Anklet.

SLOUCH BEANIE

So simple to make, the Slouch Beanie is also a trendy design for fashion-forward adults.

■□□□ BEGINNER

Finished Size: Adult

SHOPPING LIST

Yarn (Medium Weight) **④**

[6 ounces, 315 yards
(170 grams, 288 meters) per skein]:

☐ 1 skein

Loom (Round)

☐ 40 Pegs

Crochet Hook

☐ Size K (6.5 mm)

Additional Supplies

☐ Knitting loom tool

☐ Yarn needle

GAUGE INFORMATION

Beanie is worked holding two strands of yarn together as one throughout. Pull one strand from the center and one from the outside of the skein.
In Stockinette Stitch (knit every rnd),
    10 stitches = 4" (10 cm) and
    14 rnds = 3" (7.5 cm)
In Twisted Stockinette Stitch
(e-wrap knit every rnd),
    9 stitches = 4" (10 cm)

INSTRUCTIONS
BAND

Holding 2 strands of yarn together and working as circular knitting, chain cast on all 40 pegs counter-clockwise.

Knit 14 rnds.

To 🎥 form the Brim, lift up the bottom edge toward the inside of the loom and place the loops from the cast on rnd over the pegs *(Fig. 1)*. There will be 2 loops on each peg.
Lift the bottom loop on each peg over the top loop and off the peg, securing the bottom edge and leaving one loop on each peg.

Fig. 1

BODY

E-wrap knit every rnd until Beanie measures approximately 9" (23 cm) from bottom edge of Brim **or** to desired length.

Cut yarn leaving a long end for sewing. Thread the yarn needle with the yarn end.

To work  gathered removal, beginning with the last peg worked, insert the yarn needle in the loop from **bottom** to **top** *(Fig. 2a)* and lift it off the peg, sliding it onto the yarn end. Repeat for each loop around the loom. With the yarn end to the **wrong** side of the project, pull the end **tightly**, gathering the loops to the center *(Fig. 2b)*. Knot the yarn **tightly** and weave in the end; clip the yarn end close to work.

Weave in beginning yarn end.

Fig. 2a

Fig. 2b

COWL

Keep that special mom comfy in a warm, close-fitting cowl.

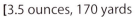 **INTERMEDIATE**

Finished Size: 5$^{1}/_{2}$" high x 18" around bottom edge (14 cm x 45.5 cm)

GAUGE INFORMATION

Cowl is worked holding two strands of yarn together as one throughout. Pull one strand from the center and one from the outside of the skein.
In EWK1, P1 ribbing,
    10 stitches = 4" (10 cm)

INSTRUCTIONS

Holding 2 strands of yarn together and working as circular knitting, chain cast on all 40 pegs counter-clockwise.

Rnd 1: Purl around.

Rnd 2: E-wrap knit around.

Rnd 3: Purl around.

Rnd 4 (Lace rnd)**:** To 🎥 set up for the decreases, work counter-clockwise and move the loop from the 5th peg to the 6th peg, (skip next 6 pegs and move the loop from the next peg to the peg on the right) 4 times, skip last 2 pegs.

🎥 Begin working the rnd: ★ EWK1, beginning with the peg before the next empty peg *(Fig. 3a)*, move the loops from the next 3 pegs one at a time to an empty peg, leaving the peg from the last loop moved empty, e-wrap the empty peg clockwise **(yarn around the peg, abbreviated YRP)** *(Fig. 3b)*, EWK2, [skip the next peg and bring the yarn to the front, knit the next peg by lifting the bottom 2 loops over the working yarn and off the peg *(Fig. 3c)*. Move the loop just made to the skipped peg. Without knitting it, lift the bottom loop over the top loop and off the peg *(Fig. 3d)* **(2-stitch decrease made)]**, move the loops from the next 2 pegs, one at a time, to the left, EWK2, YRP; repeat from ★ around.

Fig. 3a

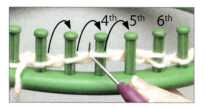

Fig. 3b

Fig. 3c

Fig. 3d

Rnd 5: E-wrap knit around.

Rnds 6-11: Repeat Rnds 4 and 5, 3 times.

Rnds 12-19: (EWK1, P1) around.

Work 🎥 chain one bind off around.

HOODED SCARF

This stylish muffler with convenient knit-in hood will turn away the cold!

■■□□□ EASY

SHOPPING LIST

Yarn (Medium Weight)

[5 ounces, 256 yards
(140 grams, 234 meters) per skein]:

☐ 2{3} skeins

Loom (Round)

☐ 30 Pegs (minimum)

Crochet Hook

☐ Size K (6.5 mm)

Additional Supplies

☐ Knitting loom tool

☐ Yarn needle

SIZE INFORMATION

Size	Finished Size
Child	7" x 45" (18 cm x 114.5 cm)
Adult	8" x 56" (20.5 cm x 142 cm)

Size Note: We have printed the instructions for the sizes in different colors to make it easier for you to find:
Child size in pink.
Adult size in green.
Instructions in black apply to both sizes.

GAUGE INFORMATION

Hooded Scarf is worked holding two strands of yarn together as one throughout.

In pattern,
    12 stitches = 3¹/₂" (9 cm) and
    16 rows = 3³/₄" (9.5 cm);
In Twisted Stockinette Stitch
(e-wrap knit every row),
    10 stitches and 14 rows = 4" (10 cm)

INSTRUCTIONS
RIGHT SCARF

Holding two strands of yarn together and working as flat knitting, chain cast on 25{28} pegs counter-clockwise.

Rows 1-3: 📹 Skip 1 *(Fig. 9, page 30)*, (EWK2, P1) across to last 3 pegs, EWK3.

Row 4: Skip 1, purl across to last peg, EWK1.

Repeat Rows 1-4, 14{18} times.

Note: The Right Scarf should measure approximately 14{18}"/35.5{45.5} cm from cast on edge.

HOOD

Row 1: Skip 1, (EWK2, P1) twice, e-wrap knit across.

Row 2: E-wrap knit across to last 7 pegs, P1, EWK2, P1, EWK3.

Row 3: Skip 1, (EWK2, P1) twice, e-wrap knit across.

Row 4: E-wrap knit across to last 7 pegs, P6, EWK1.

Repeat Rows 1-4, 13{16} times; then repeat Rows 1-3 once **more**.

Note: The Hood should measure approximately 17{20}"/43{51} cm.

LEFT SCARF

Row 1: Skip 1, purl across to last peg, EWK1.

Rows 2-4: Skip 1, (EWK2, P1) across to last 3 pegs, EWK3.

Repeat Rows 1-4, 14{18} times.

Note: The Left Scarf should measure the same as the Right Scarf.

Work  chain one bind off across.

FINISHING

Fold piece in half, matching first and last row on Hood. Beginning at bottom of Hood, weave end of rows together across Twisted Stockinette Stitch section to form the back seam *(Fig. 13, page 31)*.

SOCK MONKEY PILLOW

The Sock Monkey Pillow is custom-made for receiving big hugs.

 **EASY +**

Finished Size: 12" x 16"
(30.5 cm x 40.5 cm)

SHOPPING LIST

Yarn (Medium Weight)
[3.5 ounces, 170 yards
(100 grams, 156 meters) per skein]:
- ☐ Grey - 2 skeins
- ☐ White - 1 skein
- ☐ Red - 1 skein

Loom (Round)
- ☐ 30 Pegs (minimum)

Crochet Hook
- ☐ Size K (6.5 mm)

Additional Supplies
- ☐ Knitting loom tool
- ☐ Yarn needle
- ☐ Pillow form - 12" x 16"
  (30.5 cm x 40.5 cm)
- ☐ Black felt (for eyes) - 2" x 4"
  (5 cm x 10 cm) piece
- ☐ Polyester fiberfill (for mouth) -
  small amount
- ☐ Craft glue

GAUGE INFORMATION

Pillow is worked holding two strands of yarn together as one throughout. When using White or Red, pull one strand from the center and one from the outside of the skein.
In Twisted Stockinette Stitch (e-wrap knit every row),
   8 stitches and 13 rows = 4" (10 cm)

INSTRUCTIONS
PILLOW BODY (Make 2)
Holding 2 strands of Grey together and working as flat knitting, chain cast on 29 pegs counter-clockwise.

Rows 1-33: E-wrap knit across.

Cut Grey and begin using 2 strands of White for beginning of hat, leaving long ends to weave in later.

When changing to the next color, 🎥 twist the yarns to create a neat edge *(Fig. 8b, page 29)*.

Rows 34 and 35: With White, E-wrap knit across.

Rows 36 and 37: With Red, purl across.

Rows 38-45: Repeat Rows 34-37 twice.

Cut Red.

Rows 46-49: With White, E-wrap knit across.

Rows 50-57: Bind off 3 pegs using 🎥 simple bind off *(Figs. 11a & b, page 30)*, E-wrap knit across: 5 pegs used.

Bind off remaining stitches using simple bind off method.

SOCK MONKEY MOUTH
The Mouth shaping is achieved by 🎥 working in short rows, formed by working across only some of the pegs. Wrap the peg indicated *(Figs. 10a & b, page 30)*, then reverse the direction you are working at the end of the instructions for each row, leaving the remaining pegs unworked.

Holding 2 strands of White together and working as flat knitting, chain cast on 20 pegs counter-clockwise.

Row 1: E-wrap knit across.

Rows 2 and 3: E-wrap knit across to last peg, wrap last peg.

Row 4: EWK 17, wrap next peg.

Row 5: EWK 16, wrap next peg.

Row 6: EWK 15, wrap next peg.

Row 7: EWK 14; drop White.

Row 8: With Red and beginning with the last peg worked, EWK 13, wrap next peg.

Row 9: EWK 12, wrap next peg.

Row 10: EWK 11, wrap next peg.

Row 11: EWK 10, wrap next peg.

Row 12: EWK9, wrap next peg.

Row 13: EWK8, wrap next peg.

Row 14: EWK7, wrap next peg.

Row 15: EWK6, wrap next peg.

To e-wrap knit a wrapped peg, e-wrap knit the peg by lifting all loops over the top loop and off the peg. **When wrapping a peg more than once**, lift the top loop from the peg and place the wrap **above** the last one, then put the loop back onto the peg. **When e-wrap knitting a peg with multiple wraps**, the loops can be lifted off, one at a time, from the bottom to the top.

Row 16: EWK 7, wrap next peg.

Row 17: EWK 8, wrap next peg.

Row 18: EWK 9, wrap next peg.

Row 19: EWK 10, wrap next peg.

Row 20: EWK 11, wrap next peg.

Row 21: EWK 12, wrap next peg.

Row 22: EWK 13, wrap next peg.

Row 23: EWK 14; cut Red.

Row 24: With White and beginning with the last peg worked, EWK 15, wrap next peg.

Row 25: EWK 16, wrap next peg.

Row 26: EWK 17, wrap next peg.

Row 27: EWK 18, wrap next peg.

Row 28: EWK 19.

Row 29: E-wrap knit across.

Loosely bind off all stitches using simple bind off method; cut yarn leaving a long end of one strand for sewing the Mouth.

SOCK MONKEY EAR (Make 4)
Holding 2 strands of Grey together and working as flat knitting, chain cast on 14 pegs counter-clockwise.

Rows 1-10: E-wrap knit across.

Bind off Row: ★ Move the loop from the first peg to the second peg, lift the bottom loop over the top loop and off the peg; repeat from ★ until one loop remains, EWK 1; cut yarn and pull end through remaining stitch pulling tightly to form a half circle.

With **wrong** sides together, sew 2 Ear pieces together along the cast on edge for each Ear.

FINISHING
With **wrong** sides together and matching rows, sew both Pillow Body pieces together, inserting the pillow form before closing.

Use photo as a guide for placement of all pieces.

Pin Mouth to Pillow Body, lightly stuffing with polyester fiberfill; sew in place using long end.

Folding each Ear along the seam and working through **both** thicknesses, sew the end of the rows to the side seam of the Pillow, placing the top of the Ears at the bottom of the hat.

Make a 2½" (6.5 cm) Red pom-pom *(Figs. 14a-c, page 31)* and sew it to the top of the hat.

Trace the eye diagram onto paper for a pattern then cut out two circles from black felt for the eyes. Glue the eyes in place slightly above the Mouth.

EYE DIAGRAM

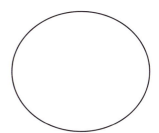

15

ELF HAT

You're sure to know a little elf who'll look adorable in this cute cap!

 **EASY**

SIZE INFORMATION

Size	Finished Circumference
Baby	12" (30.5 cm)
Child/Adult Small	14¹/₂" (37 cm)
Adult Medium/Large	16" (40.5 cm)

Size Note: We have printed the instructions for the sizes in different colors to make it easier for you to find:

Baby size in pink

Child/Adult Small size in blue

Adult Medium/Large size in green

Instructions in black apply to all sizes.

GAUGE INFORMATION

Hat is worked holding two strands of yarn together as one throughout. Pull one strand from the center and one from the outside of the skein.

In Twisted Stockinette Stitch (e-wrap knit every row/rnd), 10 stitches and 14 rows/rnds = 4" (10 cm)

STITCH GUIDE

🎥 LEFT E-WRAP DECREASE

Use the tool to move the loop from peg A to the **left** and place it on peg B, leaving peg A empty *(Fig. 4)*. E-wrap peg B and lift the bottom 2 loops over the top loop and off the peg.

Fig. 4

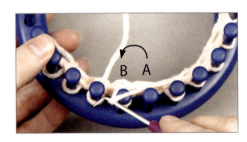

🎥 RIGHT E-WRAP DECREASE

Use the tool to move the loop from peg B to the **right** and place it on peg A, leaving peg B empty *(Fig. 5)*. E-wrap peg A and lift the bottom 2 loops over the top loop and off the peg.

Fig. 5

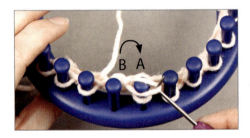

INSTRUCTIONS
BAND

Holding 2 strands of Dk Red together and working as circular knitting, chain cast on all 30{36-40} pegs counter-clockwise.

E-wrap knit 6{8-8} rnds.

The bottom edge will naturally roll, forming the brim.

BODY

The Body is made by alternating 2 rounds of each color, without cutting the yarn.

Drop Dk Red to the inside of the loom and begin using 2 strands of Off-White, leaving a long end to weave in later.

When changing to the next color, 📹 twist the yarns to prevent long strands across the back of each stripe *(Figs. 8a & b, page 29)*.

Rnds 1 and 2: With Off-White, e-wrap knit around.

Rnds 3 and 4: With Dk Red, e-wrap knit around.

Repeat Rnds 1-4, 5{6-7} times.

FIRST WEDGE

The shaping is achieved by working two separate Wedges that will be sewn together. Each Wedge is worked as flat knitting, decreasing stitches until only a few stitches are left.

Row 1: With Off-White and working in the same direction as last rnd, e-wrap knit 15{18-20} pegs.

Row 2: E-wrap knit 15{18-20} pegs.

Row 3 (Decrease row)**:** With Dk Red, right e-wrap decrease, e-wrap knit across to last 2 pegs on Wedge, left e-wrap decrease: 13{16-18} pegs remaining.

Row 4: E-wrap knit across Wedge.

Rows 5 and 6: With Off-White, e-wrap knit across Wedge.

Repeat Rows 3-6, 4{6-7} times: 5{4-4} pegs remaining.

Next Row: With Dk Red, right e-wrap decrease, e-wrap knit 1{0-0} pegs *(see Zeros, page 29)*, left e-wrap decrease: 3{2-2} pegs remaining.

Next Row: E-wrap knit 3{2-2} pegs.

Size Child/Adult Small ONLY - Last 2 Rows: With Off-White, e-wrap knit 2 pegs.

All Sizes: Cut both colors leaving one long end for sewing on the last color used. Thread the yarn needle with the yarn end. Beginning with the last peg worked, and inserting the yarn needle from **bottom** to **top**, lift each stitch off the pegs, sliding them onto the yarn end. Gather **tightly** to close and secure end.

SECOND WEDGE

Beginning with the next peg to the right of the First Wedge and leaving a long end for sewing, work same as first Wedge.

FINISHING

Using the long end at the beginning of the Second Wedge and matching stripes, 📹 weave the end of the rows of both Wedges together across both edges *(Fig. 13, page 32)*.

Make a 2" (5 cm) Dk Red 📹 pom-pom and sew it to the top of the Hat *(Figs. 14a-c, page 31)*.

JACKET

So simple and so sweet, this baby jacket will be worn and loved for generations.

Shown on page 21.

 **EASY**

SHOPPING LIST

Yarn (Medium Weight)
[5 ounces, 256 yards
(142 grams, 234 meters) per skein]:
- 1{1-1-2} skein(s)

Loom (Straight)
- 50 or 62 Pegs

Crochet Hook
- Size K (6.5 mm)

Additional Supplies
- Knitting loom tool
- 1½" (38 mm) Button
- Sewing needle
- Matching thread
- Yarn needle
- Rust-proof pins (for blocking)
- Optional: ⅞" (22 mm) wide grosgrain ribbon - 14" (35.5 cm)

SIZE INFORMATION

Size	Finished Chest Measurement
6 months	19" (48.5 cm)
12 months	20" (51 cm)
24 months	22" (56 cm)
3 years	24" (61 cm)

Size Note: We have printed the instructions for the sizes in different colors to make it easier for you to find:

6 months Size in green

12 months Size in red

24 months Size in purple

3 years Size in blue

Instructions in black apply to all sizes.

GAUGE INFORMATION

In Stockinette Stitch (knit every row),
16 stitches and 20 rows = 4" (10 cm)

——— STITCH GUIDE ———

YRP, LEFT DECREASE

On a right to left row, use the tool to move the loop from peg A to the **left** and place it on peg B, leaving peg A empty *(Fig. 6)*. E-wrap the empty peg counter-clockwise *(yarn around the peg, abbreviated YRP)*, and bring the yarn to the outside. Knit the next peg lifting the bottom 2 loops over the working yarn and off the peg to create the decrease.

Fig. 6

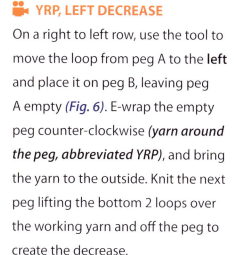

INSTRUCTIONS

The Jacket is worked in one piece, beginning at the bottom edge of the Back. The Right Front is worked from the shoulder to the bottom edge without removing the Back stitches from the loom. The process is repeated for the Left Front. The Sleeves are worked separately.

BACK
RIBBING

Working as flat knitting, chain cast on 40{42-46-50} pegs counter-clockwise.

Row 1: (K1, P1) across.

Row 2: (P1, K1) across.

Repeat Rows 1 and 2 for 1" (2.5 cm).

BODY

Knit every row until Back measures approximately 9$\frac{1}{2}${10$\frac{1}{2}$-11$\frac{1}{2}$-13}"/24{26.5-29-33} cm from cast on edge, ending with the working yarn on the left-hand edge.

Neck Bind Off: K 10{10-11-12} and leave stitches on pegs for Left Front; bind off next 20{22-24-26} pegs for neck, knit across for Right Front: 10{10-11-12} pegs remaining on **each** side of neck.

RIGHT FRONT
BODY

Row 1: K 10{10-11-12}, chain cast on 12{13-14-15} pegs clockwise: 22{23-25-27} pegs used.

Row 2: (K1, P1) twice, knit across.

Row 3 (Buttonhole row)**:** Knit across to last 4 pegs, YRP, left decrease, K2.

Row 4: (K1, P1) twice, knit across.

Row 5: Knit across to last 4 pegs, (P1, K1) twice.

Repeat Rows 4 and 5 until Right Front measures approximately 8$\frac{1}{2}${9$\frac{1}{2}$-10$\frac{1}{2}$-12}"/21.5{24-26.5-30.5} cm from neck bind off, ending with the working yarn on the left-hand edge.

RIBBING

Row 1: (K1, P1) across to last 0{1-1-1} peg *(see Zeros, page 29)*, K 0{1-1-1}.

Row 2: K 0{1-1-1}, (P1, K1) across.

Repeat Rows 1 and 2 for 1" (2.5 cm).

Work 🎥 chain one bind off across.

LEFT FRONT
BODY

Row 1: Beginning on left edge, K 10{10-11-12}, chain cast on 12{13-14-15} pegs counter-clockwise: 22{23-25-27} pegs used.

Row 2: (K1, P1) twice, knit across.

Row 3: Knit across to last 4 pegs, (P1, K1) twice.

Repeat Rows 2 and 3 until Left Front measures same as Right Front, ending with the working yarn on the right-hand edge.

RIBBING

Row 1: (K1, P1) across to last 0{1-1-1} peg, K 0{1-1-1}.

Row 2: K 0{1-1-1}, (P1, K1) across.

Repeat Rows 1 and 2 for 1" (2.5 cm).

Work chain one bind off across.

SLEEVE (Make 2)
RIBBING

Working as flat knitting, chain cast on 32{36-40-44} pegs counter-clockwise.

Row 1: (K1, P1) across.

Row 2: (P1, K1) across.

Repeat Rows 1 and 2 for 1" (2.5 cm).

BODY

Knit every row until Sleeve measures approximately 4$\frac{1}{2}${5$\frac{1}{2}$-6$\frac{1}{2}$-7$\frac{1}{2}$}"/11.5{14-16.5-19} cm from cast on edge.

Work chain one bind off across.

FINISHING

Fold the Jacket in half to identify the shoulders and place markers (using short pieces of yarn) at each shoulder and 4{4¹/₂-5-5¹/₂}"/ 10{11.5-12.5-14} cm down from shoulders on Fronts and Back. Sew Sleeves to Body, placing center of top edge on Sleeve at shoulder and edges at markers.

🎥 Weave underarm and side in one continuous seam *(Fig. 13, page 31)*.

Block Jacket as follows: Check the yarn label for any special instructions about blocking. With acrylics that can be blocked, place your project on a clean terry towel over a flat surface and pin in place to the desired size using rust-proof pins where needed. Cover it with dampened bath towels. When the towels are dry, the project is blocked.

Sew Button to Front opposite buttonhole.

To add stability to the front edge, ⁷/₈" (22 mm) wide grosgrain ribbon can be hand stitched to the wrong side. To add stability to the neckline, a slip stitch or single crochet edging can be added.

FINGERLESS MITTS

These handy texting mitts unfold to keep fingers cozy between messages.

 **EASY**

Finished Hand Circumference:
    6½" (16.5 cm)

SHOPPING LIST

Yarn (Medium Weight)
[1.75 ounces, 147 yards
(50 grams, 135 meters) per skein]:
☐ 1 skein
Loom (Straight)
☐ 26 Pegs
Crochet Hook
☐ Size K (6.5 mm)
Additional Supplies
☐ Knitting loom tool
☐ Yarn needle

Sizing Note: The weight and type of yarn that you use (whether it's soft or has more body) and the tension of your yarn wraps will greatly effect your gauge and thus the finished size. Therefore, you can easily adjust the size of your mitts by the yarn you choose and your tension.

GAUGE INFORMATION
In Stockinette Stitch
(knit every row/rnd),
    16 stitches and 24 rows/rnds =
    4" (10 cm)

INSTRUCTIONS
THUMB
Working as flat knitting and beginning with peg 23 *(see diagram, page 23)*, chain cast on 9 pegs counter-clockwise, ending with peg 5.

Row 1: Knit across.

Row 2: Purl across.

Rows 3-6: Knit across.

Cut yarn; do **not** remove stitches from pegs.

HAND
Beginning with peg 6 and leaving a long end for sewing, chain cast on remaining 17 pegs counter-clockwise.

Work as flat knitting across 17 Hand pegs only.

Row 1: Knit across.

Row 2: Purl across.

Rows 3-16: Repeat Rows 1 and 2, 7 times.

Rows 17-26: Knit across.

JOIN HAND TO THUMB
Begin working as circular knitting.

Rnd 1: Place a scrap piece of yarn around peg 22 to mark the end of a round; beginning with Thumb peg 23, knit all 26 pegs.

Rnds 2-15: Knit around.

RIBBING
Rnds 1-9: (K1, P1) around.

Work 📹 sewn bind off *(Figs. 12a & b, page 31)*.

📹 Weave seam along inside of Hand and Thumb *(Fig. 13, page 31)*.

Repeat for second Mitt.

Refer to the diagram for the numbering system used in this pattern.

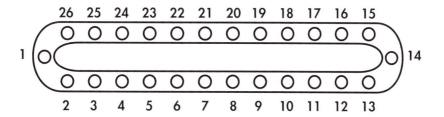

BABY SOCKS

It's so easy to make these socks for the newest member of the family!

Finished Size: 4" (10 cm) foot circumference and 3¹/₂" (9 cm) foot length

SHOPPING LIST

Yarn (Light Weight)

Striped Socks:
- ☐ Main Color - 35 yards (32 meters)
- ☐ Contrasting Color - 15 yards (14 meters)
- ☐ Waste yarn - small amount

Ruffled Socks:
- ☐ Main Color - 75 yards (70 meters)
- ☐ Waste yarn - small amount

Loom (Round)
- ☐ 12 Pegs (Flower loom) - both
- ☐ 24 Pegs (Ruffled Socks Only)

Crochet Hook
- ☐ Size K (6.5 mm) (Ruffled Socks Only)

Additional Supplies
- ☐ Knitting loom tool
- ☐ Yarn needle

GAUGE INFORMATION

Except for the provisional cast on, both socks are worked holding 2 strands of yarn together as one. Pull one strand from the center and one from the outside of the skein.

In Stockinette Stitch (knit every row/rnd), using Main Color,

  12 stitches = 4" (10 cm) and
  18 rows/rnds = 3" (7.5 cm)

INSTRUCTIONS
Striped & Ruffled Socks

These socks are a toe up pattern. A single strand of waste yarn is used for the provisional cast on and also to aid in joining the ruffle to the ribbing.

PROVISIONAL CAST ON

Using the 12 peg flower loom, a single strand of waste yarn, and working as flat knitting, e-wrap cast on 6 pegs counter-clockwise.

E-wrap knit 3 rows.

Cut waste yarn.

TOE SHAPING

Use the knit stitch (instead of the e-wrap knit stitch) unless otherwise indicated.

Row 1: Holding 2 strands of Main Color together, knit across.

Row 2: Knit across.

Row 3: Knit across, e-wrap next empty peg (counter-clockwise around the peg): 7 pegs used.

Row 4: Skip first peg, K6, e-wrap next empty peg (clockwise around the peg): 8 pegs used.

The Toe shaping is achieved by 📹 working in short rows, formed by working across only some of the pegs. Wrap the peg indicated *(Figs. 10a & b, page 30)*, then reverse the direction you are working at the end of the instructions for each row, leaving the remaining pegs unworked.

Row 5: Skip first peg, K5, wrap next peg.

Row 6: K4, wrap next peg.

Row 7: K3, wrap next peg.

Row 8: K2, wrap next peg.

To knit a wraped peg, knit the peg by lifting all loops over the working yarn and off the peg. **When wrapping a peg more than once**, lift the top loop from the peg and place the wrap **above** the last one, then put the loop back onto the peg. **When knitting a peg with multiple wraps**, the loops can be lifted off, one at a time, from the bottom to the top.

Row 9: K3, wrap next peg.

Row 10: K4, wrap next peg.

Row 11: K5, wrap next peg.

Row 12: K6, wrap next peg.

Row 13: K6.

Lift up the bottom edge toward the inside of the loom and  place the loops from first row of Main Color on the pegs, placing the end stitches on the same pegs as the first and last pegs used and the 4 center stitches on the 4 empty pegs *(Figs. 7a & b, page 29)*; remove waste yarn: 12 pegs used.

Row 14: Continuing to work in the same direction as the previous row, knit the next peg and lift all loops over working yarn and off peg, K4, knit next peg and lift all loops over working yarn and off peg.

FOOT
Begin working as circular knitting.

Knit 10 rounds.

Striped Socks Only
HEEL
Drop Main Color to the inside of the loom and begin using 2 strands of Contrasting Color, leaving a long end to weave in later.

Begin working in short rows.

Row 1: K5, wrap next peg.

Row 2: K4, wrap next peg.

Row 3: K3, wrap next peg.

Row 4: K2, wrap next peg.

Row 5: K3, wrap next peg.

Row 6: K5; drop Contrasting Color.

RIBBING
Begin working as circular knitting.

When changing to the next color, twist the yarns to prevent long strands across the back of each stripe *(Figs. 8a & b, page 29)*.

Rnds 1 and 2: With Main Color, (K1, P1) around.

Rnds 3 and 4: With Contrasting Color, (K1, P1) around.

Rnds 5-8: Repeat Rnds 1-4.

Cut Main Color.

Using Contrasting Color, work

sewn bind off *(Figs. 12a & b, page 31)*.

Repeat for second Sock.

Ruffled Socks Only
HEEL
Begin working in short rows.

Row 1: K5, wrap next peg.

Row 2: K4, wrap next peg.

Row 3: K3, wrap next peg.

Row 4: K2, wrap next peg.

Row 5: K3, wrap next peg.

Row 6: K4, wrap next peg.

Row 7: K 11.

RIBBING

Begin working as circular knitting.

Rnd 1: Knit first peg and lift all loops over working yarn and off peg, P1, (K1, P1) around.

Rnds 2-9: (K1, P1) around.

Cut Main Color.

Rnds 10 and 11: Using a single strand of waste yarn, e-wrap knit around.

Work  simple bind off *(Figs. 11a & b, page 30)*.

RUFFLE

Using the 24 peg round loom and holding 2 strands of Main Color together, chain cast on all 24 pegs counter-clockwise.

Rnd 1: (K1, P1) around.

Rnd 2: (P1, K1) around.

Rnd 3: (K1, P1) around.

Rnd 4: Knit around; drop Main Color (to be used when joining Ruffle to Ribbing).

Rnds 5 and 6: Using a single strand of waste yarn, e-wrap knit around.

JOINING RUFFLE TO RIBBING

The Ruffle needs to be moved to the 12 peg flower loom. Carefully remove the stitches from the pegs, then insert the Ruffle inside the flower loom. Transferring stitches from last round of Main Color (Rnd 4), place 2 stitches onto each peg; remove waste yarn: 12 pegs used.

Rnd 1: Knit around, lifting the bottom 2 loops over the working yarn.

Rnd 2: Knit around.

Insert the Ribbing inside the flower loom. Transferring stitches from last round of Main Color (Rnd 9), place a stitch onto each peg. Remove waste yarn.

Lift the bottom loops over the top loops to join pieces.

Work sewn bind off *(Figs. 12a & b, page 31)*.

Repeat for second Sock.

27

GENERAL INSTRUCTIONS

ABBREVIATIONS

cm	centimeters
EWK	e-wrap knit
K	knit
mm	millimeters
P	purl
Rnd(s)	Round(s)
YRP	yarn around peg

SYMBOLS & TERMS

★ — work instructions following ★ as many **more** times as indicated in addition to the first time.

( ) or [ ] — work enclosed instructions **as many** times as specified by the number immediately following **or** contains explanatory remarks.

colon (:) — the number(s) given after a colon at the end of a row or round denote(s) the number of pegs you should have occupied at the end of that row or round.

working yarn — the strand coming from the skein.

GAUGE

Exact gauge is essential for proper size. Before beginning your project, make a sample swatch with the yarn and loom specified in the individual instructions. After completing the swatch, give it a tug, holding the cast on and bound off edges, then let it "rest."

Measure it, counting your stitches and rows carefully. If your swatch is larger or smaller than specified, make another, changing your tension of the working yarn as you form the stitches. Keep trying until you find the tension you need to achieve gauge. Maintain established gauge throughout project.

Yarn Weight Symbol & Names	SUPER FINE 1	FINE 2	LIGHT 3	MEDIUM 4	BULKY 5	SUPER BULKY 6
Type of Yarns in Category	Sock, Fingering, Baby	Sport, Baby	DK, Light Worsted	Worsted, Afghan, Aran	Chunky, Craft, Rug	Bulky, Roving

■□□□ BEGINNER	Projects for first-time loom knitters using basic knit and purl stitches, and simple color changes.
■■□□ EASY	Projects using basic stitches, repetitive stitch patterns, simple color changes, and simple shaping and finishing.
■■□□ EASY +	Projects using basic stitches, repetitive stitch patterns, simple color changes, simple short rows, and simple shaping and finishing.
■■■□ INTERMEDIATE	Projects with a variety of stitches, such as lace, also short rows, and mid-level shaping and finishing.

ZEROS

To consolidate the length of a pattern, zeros are sometimes used so that all of the sizes can be combined. For example, e-wrap knit 1{0-0} pegs, means that the first size would e-wrap knit one peg and the next 2 sizes would do nothing.

PROVISIONAL CAST ON

A provisional cast on is just a temporary cast on that uses a different color yarn than your project, referred to as "waste yarn." It is mainly used on toe-up sock patterns. After the toe shaping has been worked, the loops from the first row of the main color (sock color) are hung on the empty pegs so that these loops can be knitted, forming the toe.

Lift up the bottom edge toward the inside of the loom *(Fig. 7a)*. The red circle shows which loop of the main color yarn you will put on a peg.

Fig. 7a

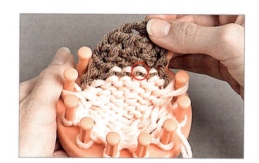

Place the end stitches on the same pegs as the first and last pegs used *(Fig. 7b)*, and the remaining stitches on the empty pegs. Remove the waste yarn.

Fig. 7b

CHANGING COLORS

When changing colors, drop the color that you are working with to the inside of the loom, then pick up the next color from underneath the strand *(Figs. 8a or b)*. This will twist the yarns to prevent long strands across the back of each stripe when working circular, or create a neat edge along your knitting when working in rows. Do **not** cut the yarn unless specified.

Fig. 8a

Fig. 8b

SKIP A PEG

Skipping the first peg of a row creates a finished look to the vertical edge of a project. Simply don't wrap or knit the peg to be skipped *(Fig. 9)*. **It is referred to as skip 1.**

Fig. 9

WRAP A PEG

Wrap the peg indicated as follows:

Step 1: Move the working yarn to the side and out of the way. Using the tool, lift the loop from the peg to be wrapped and hold it on the tool.

Step 2: Bring the working yarn behind the empty peg, then to the outside of the loom and across the front of the empty peg *(Fig. 10a, shown working a row from left to right)*.

Fig. 10a

Step 3: Put the loop back onto the peg. The wrap will be under the loop *(Fig. 10b)*.

Fig. 10b

When working the e-wrap knit stitch method, bring the working yarn back to the inside of the loom so that it is in position to work back in the other direction.

ADDITIONAL BIND OFF METHODS
SIMPLE BIND OFF

Step 1: Knit or e-wrap knit the first and second pegs.

Step 2: Use the tool to remove the loop from the peg just worked and place it on the first peg, leaving the second peg empty *(Fig. 11a)*. Lift the bottom loop over the top loop and off the peg *(Fig. 11b)*. Move the loop from the first peg back to the second peg.

Fig. 11a

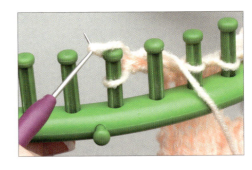

Fig. 11b

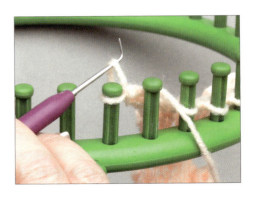

Step 3: Knit or e-wrap knit the next peg.

To bind off only a few stitches, repeat Steps 2 and 3 until the specified number of stitches have been bound off.

To bind off all stitches, repeat Steps 2 and 3 until 2 loops remain. Use the tool to remove the loop from the peg just worked and place it on the previous peg. Cut the yarn and pull the end through the final loop.

SEWN BIND OFF

Wrap the working yarn around the entire loom 3 times and cut the yarn at that point, giving you a long enough yarn to work the bind off. Unwrap the loom and thread the yarn needle with the end.

Step 1: Bring the yarn needle down through the loop on the first peg, then down through the loop on the second peg *(Fig. 12a)*.

Fig. 12a

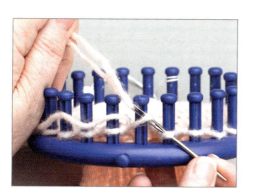

Step 2: Bring the yarn needle up through the loop on the first peg and lift it off the peg *(Fig. 12b)*, sliding it onto the yarn.

Fig. 12b

Repeat Steps 1 and 2 until one loop remains. Bring the yarn needle up through the loop on the remaining peg and lift it off the peg, pulling the yarn end through the loop.

WEAVING SEAMS

With the **right** side of both pieces facing you and edges even, sew through both sides once to secure the beginning of the seam. Insert the needle under the bar between the first and second stitches on the row and pull the yarn through *(Fig. 13)*. Insert the needle under the next bar on the second side. Repeat from side to side, being careful to match rows. If the edges are different lengths, it may be necessary to insert the needle under two bars at one edge.

Fig. 13

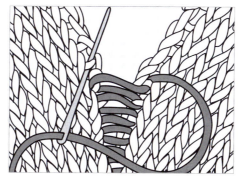

POM-POM

Cut a piece of cardboard 3" (7.5 cm) wide and as long as you want the diameter of your finished pom-pom to be.

Wind the yarn around the cardboard until it is approximately $\frac{1}{2}$" (12 mm) thick in the middle *(Fig. 14a)*. Carefully slip the yarn off the cardboard and firmly tie an 18" (45.5 cm) length of yarn around the middle *(Fig. 14b)*. Leave yarn ends long enough to attach the pom-pom. Cut the loops on both ends and trim the pom-pom into a smooth ball *(Fig. 14c)*.

Fig. 14a

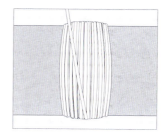

Fig. 14b

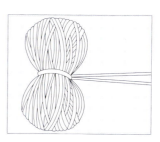

Fig. 14c

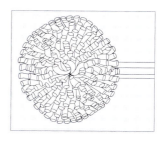

YARN INFORMATION

The items in this leaflet were made using Light Weight and Medium Weight Yarn. Any brand of the specific weight of yarn may be used. It is best to refer to the yardage/meters when determining how many balls or skeins to purchase. Remember, to arrive at the finished size, it is the GAUGE/TENSION that is important, not the brand of yarn. For your convenience, listed below are the specific yarns used to create our photography models.

ANKLETS
Bernat® Mosaic
#44309 Fantasy

SLOUCH BEANIE
Caron® Simply Soft®
#9758 Forest Floor

COWL
Lion Brand® Vanna's Choice®
#113 Scarlet

HOODED SCARF
Red Heart® Soft
9520 Seafoam

SOCK MONKEY PILLOW
Lion Brand® Vanna's Choice®
Grey - #149 Silver Grey
White - #100 White
Red - #113 Scarlet

ELF HAT
Red Heart® Designer Sport™
Color A - #3770 Berry
Color B - #3101 Ivory

JACKET
Red Heart® Soft Baby Steps™
#9620 Baby Green

FINGERLESS MITTS
Lion Brand® Amazing®
#200 Aurora

BABY SOCKS
Striped
Lion Brand® Baby Soft®
Color A - #170 Pistachio
Color B - #100 White
Ruffled
Lion Brand® Baby Soft®
#143 Lavender

We have made every effort to ensure that these instructions are accurate and complete. We cannot, however, be responsible for human error, typographical mistakes, or variations in individual work.

Production Team: Writer/Technical Editor - Cathy Hardy; Editorial Editor - Susan McManus Johnson; Senior Graphic Artist - Lora Puls; Graphic Artist - Beccas Snider Tally, Jessica Bramlett, and Stacy Owens; Photo Sylist - Brooke Duszota; and Photographer - Jason Masters.

Your opinion matters!

WE WOULD LOVE TO HEAR if our online video instructions and the new format of our publications are helpful to you!

PLEASE SHARE your comments and suggestions at www.facebook.com/Official.LeisureArts